WILDLIFE
of Southern Africa

Carol Polich

SOUTHERN AFRICA

CONTENTS

INTRODUCTION

The natural heritage of southern Africa is one of the region's most coveted treasures, and southern African countries are committed to protecting this wealth through national parks and conservancies. The region is home to an abundance of big game, birds, antelope and numerous small animals. And, as with most things, the closer you look, the more you see.

Wildlife of Southern Africa offers a photographic journey that transports you to the centre of the action: where lions roar and vultures wait patiently; where troops of baboons riot and leopards hunt alone. Here, survival is a ruthless game that targets the weak and challenges the powerful; a game in which a turn in the wind brings the smell of death and a single mistake has an immediate – and often fatal – penalty.

Despite the daily struggles of survival, most animals find time to relax. A pride of lions, after a hearty feast, finds a good spot in the shade to take a nap. Their young cubs exhaust themselves wrestling, stalking beetles and annoying their mothers by nipping at their ears and pouncing on their tails. At the waterhole, elephants indulge in spa treatments that include mud baths and icy showers. Against this apparently peaceful canvas, antelope, zebras and wildebeest mingle nervously around the waterhole, stuck in a no-man's-land between thirst and danger. Metres from them, crocodiles lie in wait for the first careless drinker.

Survival is the silent hope of the wildlife of southern Africa: wildlife of astonishing variety – immense and minute, fragile and forceful, ruthless and protective. What a privilege it is to be able to appreciate the living treasure of southern Africa's animals as they play out their lives in the freedom of their natural habitat.

The embodiment of strength and patience, a lone leopard gazes into the African sunset. As leopards prefer to hunt at night, their kills are seldom witnessed. This leopard used the cover of the photographer's vehicle and the low light conditions to get closer to its prey.

Physical touch – grooming, playing and nurturing – strengthens baboons' familial bonds. Here a young baboon gives an older sibling a pat on the head.

FAMILY AFFAIRS

Family bonds play an important role in the wild. These bonds grow stronger when animals show affection and groom one another, and when young animals play together and mimic older family members. Larger animals such as rhinoceroses fiercely protect their young against predators; the young of other creatures rely on protection from the group. Many bird species mate for life and are energetic and doting parents – even when their chicks turn out to be the progeny of other species such as the cuckoo, which lays its eggs in other birds' nests.

A lioness licks her lips as she and her cub watch the goings-on around them in the Okavango. Cubs take their cues from their mothers, learning how and where to hunt – and when to leave well alone.

The white, or square-lipped, rhinoceros is less bad-tempered and more sociable than its black, or hook-lipped, cousin. Here, a mother gently nudges her baby in a display of maternal bonding.

Masked Weavers live in colonies, with their nests suspended from reeds or tree branches.

White-fronted Bee-eaters are a common sight along the Okavango River in northwest Botswana. Gregarious birds, they live in intimate clusters, their nest holes often lining the mud banks next to rivers.

A baby baboon looks pensive as it hitches a ride on its mother's back, using her tail as a convenient backrest.

The jackal's grooming of her young pup, apart from ridding it of parasites, serves to strengthen the familial bonds between them.

Klipspringers choose one partner for life, and the pair produces a single lamb each year.

A female hyaena tries to take a nap while her young pup investigates.

In typical canine fashion, two young Cape foxes nuzzle and lick each other as a sign of affection. The only true foxes in the subregion, they eat insects and other small creatures such as rodents and birds, and even wild fruit.

It is well documented that elephants experience a range of emotions, including grief and empathy. Here, two calves use their trunks in a show of brotherly affection.

Male lions often endure being teased by the pride's cubs, but they have short tempers. Here, a cub is pushing its luck.

With its striking red eyepatches and throat pouch, the Southern Ground Hornbill is easy to identify in the wild. Its eyes are framed by impressive eyelashes, which are in fact modified feathers.

UP CLOSE

The eyes are the windows to the soul. Up close, the cheetah's gaze shows its determination and patience. The warthog tries to stare down any opposition before using its formidable weaponry – its short, powerful tusks. Sometimes, the camera's focus is boldly eye-to-eye; at other times, it captures the majestic curve of a tusk or the ferocious gape of a crocodile. Up close, the most fearsome creatures seem capable of emotion, even wisdom. These images show us intimate moments with some of nature's great personalities.

With its body adapted to hunt at full stretch, the cheetah can reach its top speed of 110 kilometres per hour in a few seconds. The black tear marks beneath its eyes help to reduce glare from the sun.

The warthog gets its name from four wart-like protrusions on its head, which – together with its formidable tusks – it uses to fight off predators and other warthogs.

Elephants use their highly specialized tusks in a variety of ways, including digging for water, stripping bark from trees and defence. Elephants are left- or right-tusked, so to speak, with one tusk used more often than the other. Tusks continue to grow throughout the elephant's life.

The leopard tortoise has a life span of about 100 years. When threatened, it withdraws into its shell and becomes inaccessible to most predators.

Puff adders start to hiss loudly and inflate their bodies if they feel threatened. They strike their prey with amazing force, the impact of which is often enough to kill the hapless victim.

With its powerful body and claws, the water monitor is a fierce hunter, as agile on land as it is in water. It is known to eat frogs, snakes, birds, crabs and rodents.

With its crown of green leaves, this lion looks the part of king of the wild. Despite its position at the top of the food chain, it is still vulnerable, owing to habitat loss and conflict with humans.

The Saddle-billed Stork is easily recognizable in the wild. Its colourful beak with a yellow 'saddle' shows up in startling contrast to the wetland environment these birds inhabit.

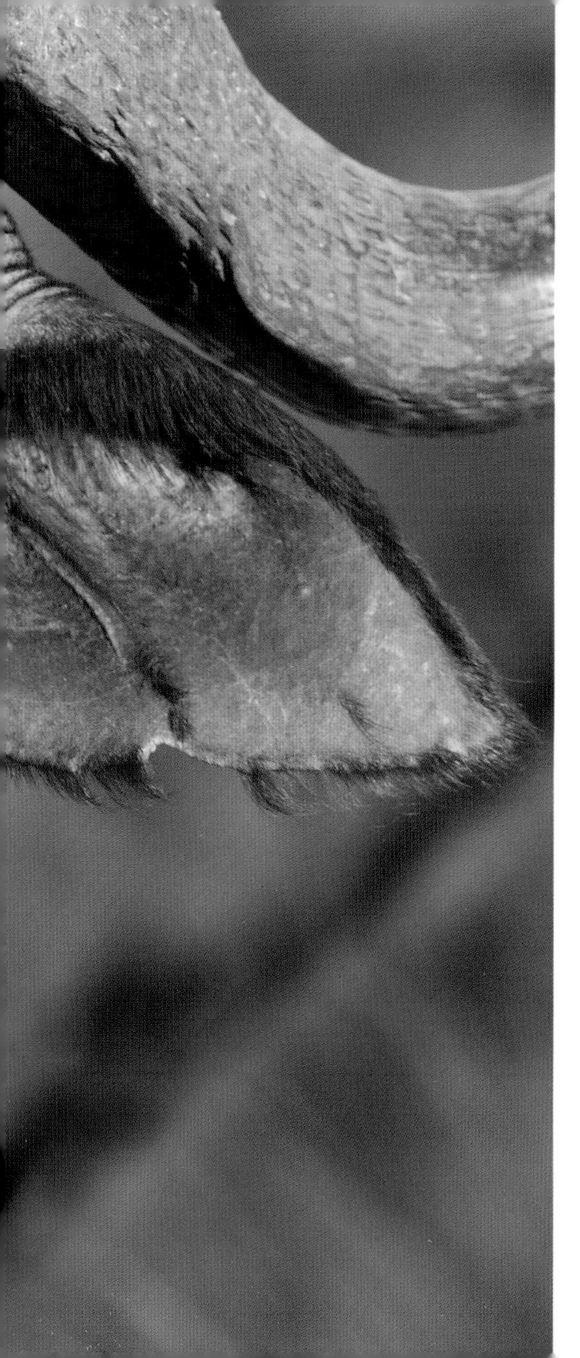

Dominating all other vultures at a kill site, the Lappet-faced Vulture uses its massive beak to open up carcasses. Usually, it does not feed directly from a carcass, but moves off by itself with a chunk of meat.

A buffalo gazes into the distance as a Red-billed Oxpecker rids it of pests.

A hippo's eyes, ears and nostrils are all situated high on its head, which allows it to keep most of its body submerged. It spends just about all its time in water, only coming onto land to feed on grass, its chief diet.

The crocodile uses its powerful jaws to pull its victim into the water, where the prey's neck is broken with a swift rolling action.

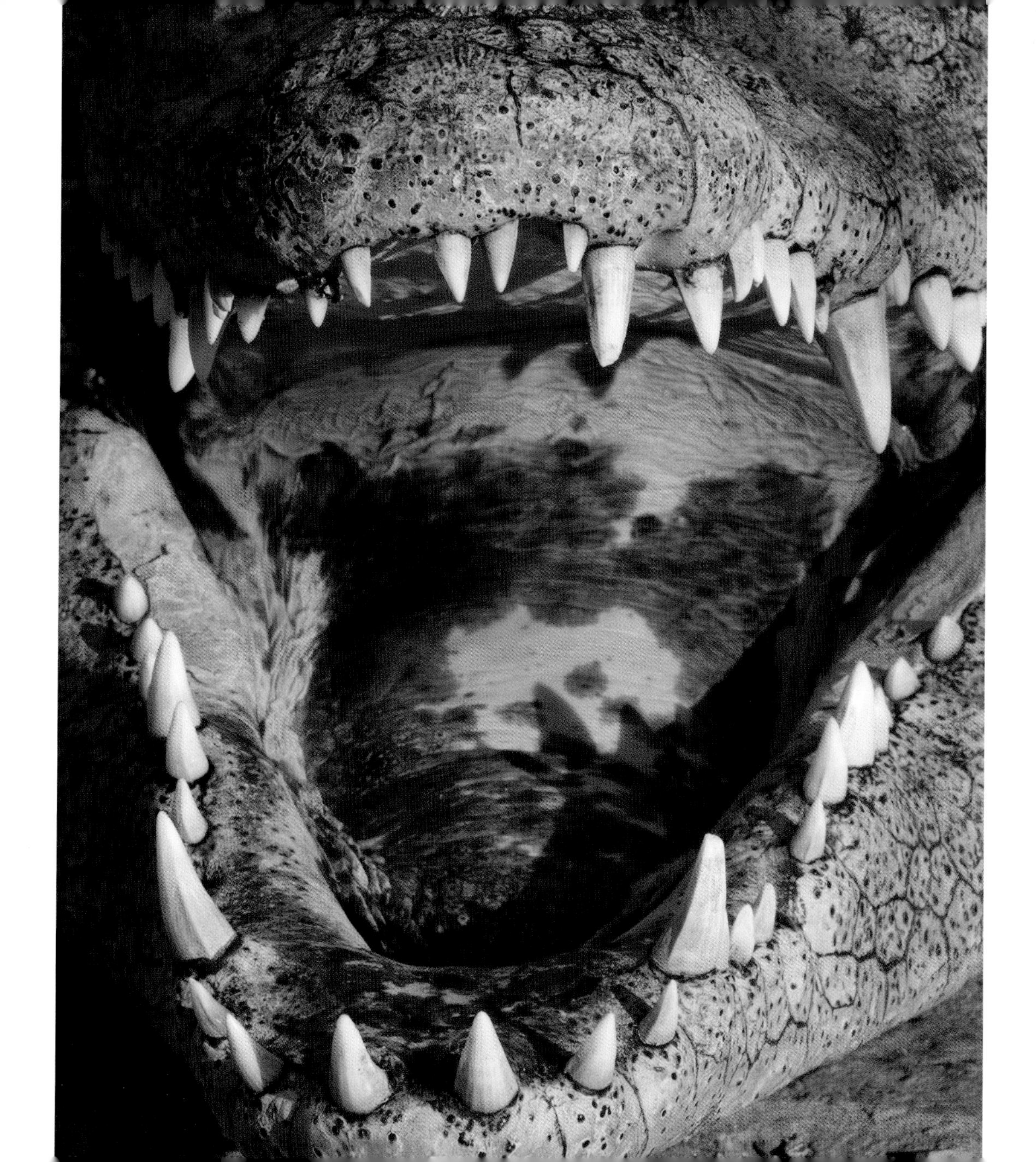

A young elephant calf reaches for a flowering bush with its dextrous trunk. Using the two finger-like projections at the end of its trunk, an elephant can pick up items as small as a single seed pod.

FINDING FOOD

Finding food dominates the lives of wild animals. Among predators, hunting styles are as varied as the creatures themselves. Some wait patiently for an opportune target, conserving energy by lying in the shade. Others actively patrol, or circle above, in the case of birds of prey, on the lookout for opportunities to launch an attack. Herbivores spend their days foraging peacefully – but always on the alert. Many graze on the long grasses of the savanna or bushveld, while those with a longer reach, such as elephants and giraffes, browse on tall trees and shrubs.

After pulling down this warthog near a parking area, a lioness – in search of some privacy – dragged her kill away from intrusive onlookers.

Water monitors eat anything they can kill (in this case, a fish).

Hyaenas are skilled and opportunistic hunters, but they also scavenge for food. Once a carcass is abandoned, they and other scavengers compete for the remains. Everything on this carcass – except for some bones and horns – will be gone within two days.

The African Darter uses its rapier-like bill to spear its meal.

A Cape Vulture steadies itself with its massive wings as it tucks into a tasty morsel at the Giant's Castle vulture 'restaurant', accompanied by a White-necked Raven.

Jackals seldom take on animals as large as this springbok, which, after falling into a waterhole, was at a disadvantage. Energized by its panic, the buck managed to escape unharmed.

Steenbok favour the leaves of woody and flowering plants, but also dig up roots and tubers. They are not dependent on drinking water, as they gain enough moisture from their food.

This male lion – the larger of two lions that attacked the impala ram – carried the carcass into the bush for a private lunch. It paused in a clearing just long enough to pose for this shot.

A giraffe curls its tongue around some juicy *Acacia* leaves and twigs. Its tongue and lips are specially adapted to withstand the plant's sharp thorns.

The Cape Rock-Jumper lives in the southwestern Cape on rocky mountain slopes, and sometimes all the way down to sea level. They can be seen in pairs or small groups, but are localized residents – and found nowhere else.

After two failed attempts, this African Fish-Eagle finally makes a catch. It grabs hold of its fish prey using its powerful claws, and flies off to a nearby perch to savour its meal.

For the sheer joy of it, three sub-adult giraffes race back and forth, kicking up dust as they go. It is a rare opportunity to see such high-spirited action among giraffes.

OFF GUARD

For game watchers, patience pays off in the wild: long, often hot, hours spent carefully observing animals in their natural habitat offer insight into survival strategies, nuances of communication and interesting social behaviours. Sustained observation may also offer a generous dose of humour as animals go about their routines and are apparently caught off guard on camera. All 'antics' are clearly within the range of common, everyday behaviour, but for the alert and quick photographer, normal becomes unusual and fascinating - and often comical.

A male Ostrich on a private game reserve displays its feathers in a territorial pose.

A dwarf mongoose looks on as its companion wakes up from a nap.

Although it seems as if they are just playing, lion cubs establish a social hierarchy through their mock fights.

Easily leaping as high as three metres into the air, the springbok uses pronking (literally 'boasting') behaviour to show off its fitness and health. When being pursued, springbok may pronk to inform predators that they are unlikely to be caught.

Face washing takes on a comical aspect as this young lion appears to hide from the camera.

Young baboons are always on the lookout for action, whether it be a wild chase or a rowdy scuffle. This youngster was caught in a quiet moment.

A zebra bares its teeth in what is an almost universal sign of aggression, used to signal both defensive and offensive modes.

Opposite: Baboon mothers are fiercely protective of their young. Here, a week-old baboon rests in the safety of its mother's lap. Above: Where the soil is lacking in potassium and phosphates – such as in Etosha National Park, Namibia – it is common to see giraffes chewing on bones.

Above: The Red-billed Oxpecker has a symbiotic relationship with several large mammals, feeding on ticks and other parasites on the animals' bodies. Opposite: A Bateleur prepares to take flight.

As one of the most intelligent creatures on earth, elephants use tools in a variety of ways. Like so many youngsters before it, this calf uses its new toy to irritate its mother.

Blue wildebeest are migratory animals, moving from the plains to relatively wetter areas when the rainy season ends. Here, a blue wildebeest bull runs to catch up with the herd.

ON THE MOVE

Effective movement is essential to survival in the wild. Predators such as cheetahs rely on their great speed to catch prey, while the herds they target must try to outrun them. Eagles glide overhead on the lookout for opportunities, soaring on rising currents of warm air. Hippos and elephants wallow in waterholes, antelope leap as they run, leopards clamber up trees and monkeys swing from branch to branch. All exude grace and power in their movements, whether they are hunting, fleeing for their lives – or simply playing.

A spirited zebra stirs up the rest of the herd.

A White-bellied Sunbird spreads its wings to take flight.

A pair of cheetahs makes haste as they position themselves for their next kill.
They will flatten out in full stride for the final sprint.

Jittery impala cross the road. With leaps of up to 10 metres, they can easily clear the single lanes in the Kruger National Park. Traffic moving along the road adds to the herd's nervousness.

Despite its size, the leopard is a proficient tree climber. It is the only wild cat that hides its prey (in this case, a warthog) in the forks of trees, away from scavengers.

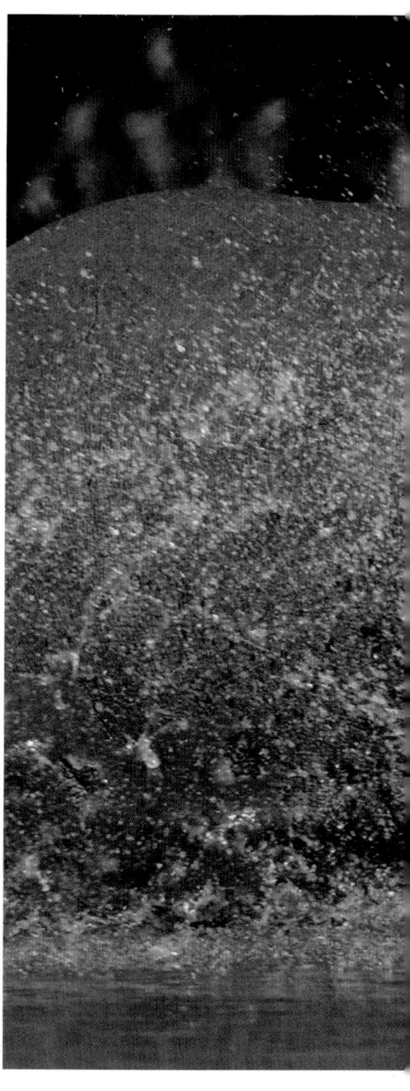

A White Pelican lands in a froth on the Walvis Bay coast. While landings and take-offs may appear clumsy, this bird soars effortlessly once aloft.

Hippos graze on land at night, and usually return to the water before full daylight. It was already mid-morning when this cow and calf raced back into the river, where the camera caught them mid-splash.

Lechwe are found in marshy habitats, such as in the Okavango, where they graze on aquatic plants. The knee–deep water offers them some form of protection from land-based predators.

A bull elephant enjoys a swim on a hot day. Apart from drinking about 100 litres of water each day, elephants wash and cool off by splashing and spraying water on their bodies with their trunks.

Creating a statuesque silhouette against the sunset, this giraffe appears frolicsome as it kicks up dust.

It is a sight and sound to behold as hundreds of queleas settle on bushes near a waterhole. En masse, they swoosh to the water's edge, drink quickly, then regroup and swarm onto nearby trees and shrubs.

A Purple-crested Turaco shakes off excess water from its bill.

A herd of nyalas comes to drink at a waterhole. In the background, a group of zebras retreats, possibly annoyed at the male nyalas' territorial displays.

THE WATERHOLE

Water is a lifeline in the African bush. Where there are pools, streams, or even the smallest of mud puddles, life can exist for another day or week. Water draws the lone leopard, busy flocks of birds and boisterous family herds, and is often the scene of great activity, especially in the cooler hours of the day. Some animals, such as zebras, are dependent on a regular intake of water. Others, such as lions and hyaenas, drink opportunistically and are able to survive for extended periods without water. More than just satisfying thirst, water offers animals the chance to bathe and cool off. A herd of elephants wallowing at a waterhole and using their versatile trunks to spray their dusty backs clean offers observers hours of entertainment.

An African Jacana and its chick walk sure-footedly on floating lily pads.

Elephants use their trunks to draw up water (as much as 10 litres), which they then deposit into their mouths for drinking.

The brightly coloured Malachite Kingfisher is a deft little hunter, in spite of its diminutive size – just 14 centimetres in length.

With its mother close by, a nyala calf prepares to take a drink.

A herd of impala comes to quench its thirst. With crocodiles being a constant threat, they seldom linger at the water's edge.

The crimson plumage of these Lesser Flamingoes is reflected in a shallow saline pan. They stamp their webbed feet to stir up the water, then use their specialized bills to separate edible particles from the mud and silt.

Despite its thick appearance, an elephant's skin is sensitive to sunburn and insect bites. Here, a young elephant stirs up the mud, which it will apply as both a sunscreen and an insect repellent.

An African Wattled Lapwing stirs things up on Lake Jozini in northern KwaZulu-Natal. The muddy plains and reed banks attract a vast array of birdlife – over 350 species have been spotted here.

To reach the level of the water, giraffes have to spread their front legs wide and stoop down low, a position that leaves them most vulnerable to attack. As this giraffe finishes its drink and jerks its head up, excess water forms an S-shaped spray.

There is a definite pecking order around waterholes. When the elephants arrive, all the other animals move away – or patiently wait their turn at a respectful distance.

The Goliath Heron is the largest of all herons and so is able to hunt for fish in deeper water.

A typically compact family of plains zebra lines up to drink. Access to water is essential for these creatures, which usually require a drink every day.

Despite the male lion's aggression, it has to wait for the female's consent before mating can take place.

DISPLAYS AND DISPUTES

The lion's roar – a statement of superiority and a chilling reminder of the predator's power and strength – is one of the most distinctive vocal displays in the African bush. Displays are also used to avoid more serious altercations. When disputes do arise, they are usually settled by one animal deferring to another, rather than by outright battles, which may result in serious injury – even a strained leg muscle can be fatal for a kudu in flight. Animals use impressive displays during mating rituals, ranging from the Ostrich's seductive dance to the giant bullfrog's distinctive call.

An adult baboon puts a youngster in its place, amidst much baring of teeth.

A Secretarybird gives chase to its prospective mate.

Two impala rams test their strength during the rutting season.

Above: Young hippos establish a social hierarchy through sparring battles. Their mouths are their main weapons and, as young bulls mature, yawning displays demonstrate their strength. Opposite: Two gemsbok engage in a battle of strength.

Opposite: In a fight, zebras can cause considerable harm with their hooves and may also attempt to bite one another in the neck. Above: This pincushion flower is clearly a prize worth fighting over; here, a Cape Sugarbird and Cape Weaver are caught in an angry exchange.

Above: Giraffes use their long and powerful necks in sparring battles and, during courtship, prospective mates will gently rub their necks together. Opposite: A young cheetah growls its displeasure at the camera.

A white rhino calf and its mother.

Published by Struik Nature
(an imprint of Random House Struik (Pty) Ltd)
Reg. No. 1966/003153/07
80 McKenzie Street, Cape Town, 8001
PO Box 1144, Cape Town, 8000 South Africa

www.randomstruik.co.za

Visit our Images of Africa website at
www.imagesofafrica.co.za

First published in 2010
1 3 5 7 9 10 8 6 4 2

ISBN 978 1 77007 846 8

Editor: Ian Parsons
Designer: Martin Endemann
Cartographer: Martin Endemann

Reproduction by Hirt and Carter Cape (Pty) Ltd
Printed and bound by Times Offset (M) Sdn Bhd
